Scholastic
Vocabulary Readers

Awesome Amphibians

Jeff Bauer

SCHOLASTIC INC.

NEW YORK • TORONTO • LONDON • AUCKLAND • SYDNEY
MEXICO CITY • NEW DELHI • HONG KONG • BUENOS AIRES

No part of this publication may be reproduced, stored in a retrieval system, or transmitted in any form or by any means, electronic, mechanical, photocopying, recording, or otherwise, without written permission of the publisher. For information regarding permission, write to Scholastic Inc., Attention: Permissions Department, 557 Broadway, New York, NY 10012.

ISBN-13: 978-0-545-06077-6 / ISBN-10: 0-545-06077-X

Photo Credits:
Cover © Gail Shumway/Getty Images; title page: © Phillippe Clement/Nature Picture Library; contents page, from top: © Ingo Arndt/Nature Picture Library, © Bob Eladale/Getty Images, © Geoff Brightling/Getty Images; page 4: © Ingo Arndt/Nature Picture Library; page 5, left: © Geoff Brightling/Getty Images; page 5, right: © Geoff Brightling/Getty Images; page 5, bottom: © Pete Oxford/Nature Picture Library; page 6, left: © Stephen Dalton/Minden Pictures; page 6, right: © Jane Burton/Nature Picture Library; page 7, left: © Jef Meul/Photo Natura/Getty Images; page 7, right: © Bernard Castelein/Nature Picture Library; page 8: © Kim Taylor/ Nature Picture Library; page 9, top left: © Bob Eladale/Getty Images; page 9, top right: © Rolf Nussbaumer/Nature Picture Library; page 9, bottom left: © Albert Lleal/Minden Pictures; page 9, bottom right: © Piotr Naskrecki/Getty Images; page 10: © Larry Minden/Minden Pictures; page 11, top left: © Kim Taylor/Nature Picture Library; page 11, top right: © Martin Harvey/Getty Images; page 11, middle left: © Don Farrell/Getty Images; page 11, middle right: © Kim Taylor/ Nature Picture Library; page 11, bottom left: © Joe Sartore/Getty Images; page 11, bottom right: © Jerry Young/Getty Images; page 12: © Michael Dick/Animals Animals; page 13: © Mark Moffett/Minden Pictures; page 14: © Kim Taylor/Nature Picture Library; page 15: © Geoff Brightling/Getty Images; back cover: © Michael Redmer/Getty Images.

Photo research by Dwayne Howard
Design by Holly Grundon

Copyright © 2009 by Lefty's Editorial Services
All rights reserved. Published by Scholastic Inc.

SCHOLASTIC and associated logos are trademarks and/or registered trademarks of Scholastic Inc.

12 11 10 9 8 7 6   10 11 12 13 14/0

Printed in the U.S.A.   40
First printing, January 2009

Contents

Chapter 1

Meet the Amphibians

alpine salamander

Check out this cool creature. It may look like a lizard, but it is not one. It is a salamander.

frog

toad

Frogs have smooth, slippery skin.

Toads have dry, warty skin.

Fast Fact

caecilian

Caecilians are amphibians, too. They spend most of their time underground.

Salamanders belong to a group of animals called amphibians. Frogs and toads are also amphibians.

Frog Life Cycle

1 Day

Female frogs lay thousands of eggs in the water.

2 Weeks

Tadpoles hatch. They live in water and breathe through gills.

All amphibians hatch from underwater eggs. At first, they need to stay in the water to survive.

3 Months

Froglets have legs. They develop lungs to breathe air.

4 Months

Grown-up frogs lose their tails. They spend a lot of time on land.

As amphibians grow, they change. After awhile, they are able to breathe air and go on land.

Chapter 2

Amphibian Skills

toad

Amphibians are **skillful** hunters. Toads use their long, sticky tongues to snatch bugs for lunch. Gotcha!

swim

hop

crawl

wiggle

Amphibians are great at getting around. Frogs and toads swim and hop. Salamanders crawl and **scurry**. Caecilians wiggle and dig.

A Pacific giant salamander hides in the woods.

Fast Fact

Birds, snakes, and raccoons all eat salamanders.

Some amphibians are great at blending in. This is called **camouflage**. Camouflage helps them hide from creatures that want to gobble them up.

yellow poison dart frog

blue poison dart frog

red-eyed tree frog

green poison dart frog

Panamanian golden frog

tomato frog

Some amphibians are great at standing out. Their bright colors warn **predators**, "Don't eat us! We taste bad and can make you sick!"

Chapter 3

Amazing Amphibians

Japanese giant salamander

Some amphibians are very large! This type of salamander can weigh more than 50 pounds. Wow!

Fast Fact

People used to think that touching frogs and toads would give them warts. But that was only a myth.

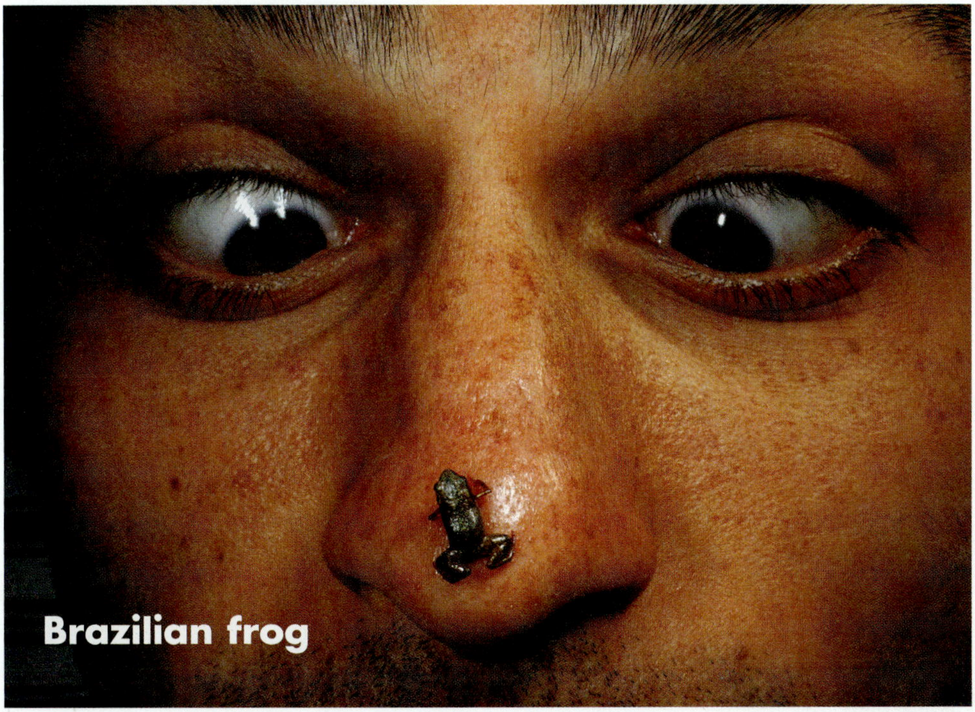
Brazilian frog

Some amphibians are tiny! This type of frog is as small as an insect.

European tree frog

Fast Fact

The world record frog long jump is 33 feet. That is longer than a bus!

Some amphibians are **exceptional** jumpers! Certain frogs can leap 20 times their body length.

ornate horned toad

Fast Fact

There are more than 5,000 different kinds of amphibians in the world.

Some amphibians are just plain funny looking! But all of them are awesome. Don't you agree?

Glossary

caecilian (se-**sil**-yen): a small wormlike amphibian that burrows in the ground

camouflage (**kam**-uh-flahzh): coloring that helps an animal blend in with its surroundings

exceptional (ek-**sep**-shuh-nuhl): great or outstanding

lungs (**luhngz**): a pair of baglike organs used to breathe air

myth (**mith**): an old story or false idea

predator (**pred**-uh-tur): an animal that lives by hunting other animals for food

scurry (**skur**-ee): to run with short, quick steps

skillful (**skil**-ful): to have skills and do something well

Comprehension Questions

1. Can you name three kinds of amphibians?

2. Can you share three facts about amphibians?

3. Which amphibian in this book is your very favorite? Tell why.